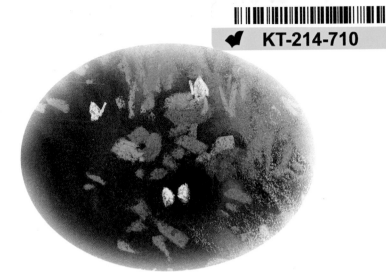

SLOWER THAN
BUTTERFLIES

Thoughts for the Day

by

EDDIE ASKEW

By the same author:

A Silence and a Shouting
Disguises of Love
Many Voices One Voice
No Strange Land
Facing the Storm
Breaking the Rules
Cross Purposes

© The Leprosy Mission International
80 Windmill Road, Brentford
Middlesex TW8 0QH, UK

© Paintings and drawings A.D. (Eddie) Askew

A.D. (Eddie) Askew has asserted his right to be identified as the author of this work in
accordance with the Copyright, Designs and Patents Act 1988

Published 1997
ISBN 0 902731 39 4
Printed by Stanley L. Hunt (Printers) Ltd, Rushden, Northants NN10 9UA

To Claudia Laurel Bell
more beautiful
than a butterfly.

Pastel paintings and drawings by the author

Foreword

Eating your cereal with one hand while making your lunch with the other ... Swigging down that cup of tea as you rush upstairs to brush your teeth, only to find that your thirteen-year-old has got there before you. These are just a few of the scenarios which I invite my 'Thought for the Day' contributors to think about as they face the daunting prospect of saying something meaningful over the airwaves at a quarter to eight on a weekday morning.

Over the past three and a half years I have spent many hours in the studio working with contributors on their thoughts. It is not easy to paint a picture using language that is easily accessible and make some sort of theological point in the space of a hundred and five seconds. Eddie does both with unfailing skill. What I most admire is that his thoughts are always open to people and to possibilities. Eddie does not preach; he reflects and, like Jesus, is able to see and appreciate God in every situation. He is comfortable with the uncomfortable. Perhaps that's the artist in him. And perhaps that explains why there are now over half a million of Eddie's books in print. His words and his paintings touch a nerve. I'm sure this latest collection will do the same.

Liz Leonard
Religious Affairs Producer
BBC Radio Nottingham

Butterflies by the river

Preface

Each of the comments in this book was written as a "*Thought for the Day*" for BBC Radio Nottingham. The time programmed for this is 1 minute 45 seconds, and not a second more. The challenge is to catch the listeners' attention, say something helpful and offer a thought to carry into the day within that time.

Most of these thoughts stand as they were read, except for the addition of a suggested Bible reading.

Thinking of the tight timing of the broadcasts, a more apt title for the collection might have been "*Faster than Dragonflies*" rather than "*Slower than Butterflies*", but I hope that readers will slow down enough to take a thought and perhaps develop it a little for themselves as they carry it through the day.

Eddie Askew
May 1997

That which was from the beginning, which we have heard, which we have seen with our eyes, which we have looked at and our hands have touched - this we proclaim concerning the Word of life.

A neighbour of mine took his family for a week's holiday on the canal. They hired a narrow boat. The weather was kind, the landscape on the river banks green and gentle. The pace of life was slow, undemanding, apart from the locks which punctuated the journey with commas rather than full stops on the way.

A few days after their return he and I were both in our drives washing our cars. I asked him about the holiday. "Great," he said, "We relaxed, watched the life around us. One day we noticed butterflies on the river bank, and realised they were travelling faster than we were. It gave us a new perspective."

Life is fast these days. There's little time for anything but the immediate demands of work and daily living. The 'human' things are in danger of being squeezed out. A popular poet of my youth, W. H. Davies, wrote:

"What is this life if full of care, we have no time to stand and stare..."

He wasn't thinking of an aimless idleness where nothing registers, but of a long look which takes in the world around us. A look which wonders and delights in the intricate beauty of butterflies and all that nature offers. It may renew our perspective and help us understand that life is more than a mad rush from one commitment to another.

St. John links it to our spiritual awareness. *"That which we have looked at"* he says, and the word means *gazed at*, taken time over. Whether it's the river bank, butterflies or the revelation of God's love in Jesus Christ, we need to take time to consider it, absorb its beauty and reflect on how it can change our lives.

A. D. ASKEW

The Word became flesh and made his dwelling among us. We have seen his glory . . .

Whenever I watch wildlife programmes on television I think of David Attenborough. He's made us so conscious of the world of nature and its wonders. Someone said that when he dies he should be put in a shoe box and buried at the bottom of the garden with the hamsters, but that's another story.

Recently I watched a programme on grey whales. Their beauty left me speechless - for a moment anyway - their twists and turns, their graceful pirouettes as they swam in and out of the picture, now close up, now disappearing into the green depths of the water.

The commentator admitted that their lives are still very private and that we know little about them. He finished by saying, "Maybe it's good that there are things we don't know. We need to keep the mystery of life."

Whatever the subject, we want to know more. That's what science is about, observing and recording, satisfying our curiosity, adding to the knowledge we already have. And that's fine, but every time we find an answer it seems to raise more questions.

The mystery's still there. Reminding us that we can never know everything, because the source, the prime mover in creation, is that power we call God. A God whom we believe is revealed to us in Jesus Christ, but even here the mystery remains. However much we know of him, there's more to learn, more to experience.

There's a time to measure and analyse, but there's also a time to sit back, accept, and say "Thank you."

Consider the lilies of the field

He answered, " 'Love the Lord your God with all your heart and with all your soul and with all your strength and with all your mind'; and, 'Love your neighbour as yourself.' "

Edward Seago's paintings are deceptively simple, and many amateur painters try to imitate his style. They quickly learn that the simplicity is the hardest thing to copy.

Seago had a great gift for analysing his subject, usually a landscape. He could identify the essentials, paint them and leave everything else out. So many painters go on adding. "I must just put another tree in there" or "I'll just go over that bit again". That's when they come to grief, and the picture loses its spontaneity. The finishing touch often does just that – finishes it off. Simplicity comes hard.

Seago suffered from chronic illness for much of his life. In early youth he was an invalid as often as not and painting became his way of using the time. For a month he drew the same tree every day until he knew just how each branch looked and responded in all weather conditions. Often, from his bed, he would paint six sky studies a day, each one helping him store up more knowledge.

It was these years of discipline which gave him that breathtaking simplicity. We admire it, envy it, but we aren't prepared for the hard work to achieve it.

The Christian faith is at its best and most effective when we allow the simplicity of Jesus' words to *"love God ... and your neighbour as yourself"* to take over. But, like painting, it's not as easy as it sounds. It takes commitment and discipline. Fortunately God's around to help us start again each time we spoil the picture.

Then Peter came to Jesus and asked, "Lord, how many times shall
I forgive my brother when he sins against me? Up to seven
times?" Jesus answered, "I tell you, not seven times, but
seventy-seven times."

Thinking about Good Friday two names spring to mind – those of
Judas and Peter. Both were followers and close friends of Jesus, and
both turned their backs on him in the crisis.

Judas betrayed Jesus to the authorities, helped them arrest him and put
him through an illegal trial that Amnesty International would shout
about today. Peter, identified as a disciple after the arrest, denied that
he'd ever known Jesus at all. "Not me," he said, "I've nothing to do
with him."

A few hours later both of them – Judas and Peter – realised how wrong
they'd been, what a mess they'd made of things. So far, they look pretty
much alike. But then came the difference.

In his despair at what he'd done, Judas plunged into a terrible
depression, went out and killed himself. Peter must have been pretty
desperate too, but he hung on, faced his problems and tried to pick up
the pieces of his life. And in due course Peter met the risen Jesus, was
forgiven, taken back into the family and given a job to do.

If only Judas had held on, found the courage and the strength to wait
and sweat it out. I reckon that if he had, he'd have been forgiven too.
In imagination I see Jesus and Judas meeting again, Jesus holding out
his arms in love as Judas earlier had held his out in betrayal, because
forgiveness has no limits.

Two ways of dealing with failure. One lets failure win, the other says
there's light at the end of the tunnel. Yes, I know the jokes about
tunnels but it's still true. Good Friday and Easter are about hope
conquering despair, and giving us all the chance to start life again.

"Anyone who has seen me has seen the Father... I am in the Father and the Father is in me" . . .

One of the many stories surrounding school nativity plays is the one in which the small shepherds, in dressing gowns and tea towels, and leading sheep covered in hearth rugs, stumble onto the stage to kneel around the baby Jesus.

The shepherds, encouraged by their teacher in rehearsal to use their own words to act out the story, are quiet for a moment. They shuffle and look at each other. Then they look at the baby. One speaks. "Oh! He does look like his dad," he says.

A phrase he'd heard his mother say as she admired a neighbour's new baby. The audience smiled, but behind the fun and the giggles there was a real truth. Jesus did look like his dad.

His whole life, his words and actions, were meant to show us what God was like. To tell us that God isn't way above the clouds in some divine shopping centre, which is as near to heaven as some of us can imagine, but is down here on earth with us, waiting to enter our lives.

Looking at Jesus we can learn a lot about love and forgiveness, and a complete commitment to other people. And when we change the looking at to following he offers us the strength to live more positively and to become more "like his dad."

"The man who enters by the gate is the shepherd of his sheep. The watchman opens the gate for him, and the sheep listen to his voice. He calls his own sheep by name and leads them out."

Walking through the city centre I saw women with clipboards, pens poised. With bright smiles they were approaching shoppers. "Just five minutes, madam, to ask you a few questions. I hope you can spare the time."

The questions they ask are wide. What newspaper do you read? Which deodorant do you use, how much chocolate do you buy each week? How much do you believe what politicians say on a scale of 1 to 10?

Sometimes I try to side-step them but I must admit they rarely stop me anyway. Even though I've no desire to share my preference in wholemeal bread with a stranger I must admit I sometimes feel a bit left out. Ignored. Why don't they stop me? Isn't my opinion valuable?

But when they do stop me they usually make it quite clear that the whole exercise is anonymous. They don't want my name or address. They're not interested in me as a person, not even as a name. I'm just another filled in form to be added to all the other filled in forms, to be fed into a computer, chewed and digested, the results tabulated and put onto a marketing manager's desk. For lunch.

Jesus describes himself as a shepherd who knows his sheep so well that he calls each of them by name. We're not just numbers to God, we're individuals, valued for what we are, not just for the bits of information we can offer to some celestial computer. Every hair on our head is numbered; our personalities respected. And we're loved infinitely by an infinite God.

And in the same passage from the gospel Jesus the shepherd offers us not an improved brand of cornflakes but new life.

As the Philistine moved closer to attack him, David ran quickly towards the battle line to meet him. Reaching into his bag and taking out a stone, he slung it and struck the Philistine on the forehead, and he fell face down on the ground.

So David triumphed over the Philistine with a sling and a stone . . .

Do you remember the story of David and Goliath? Goliath's the baddy, a giant soldier stronger than anyone else. David's a shepherd boy, the young hero who, with great courage and faith in his God, went out with a sling and hit the giant in the forehead with a stone. Exit giant, minus head.

I used to find that story a bit hard to believe. Killing a strong man with a small stone seemed unlikely. Then I visited the British Museum in London. They've got sling stones there that were dug up in Israel by archaeologists. They're as big as cricket balls – the stones, not the archaeologists – and thrown expertly by a sling can travel at a hundred miles an hour. That could change the face of cricket. It certainly changed the face of Goliath.

The Bible tells us that when David first saw Goliath David was up on a hillside, Goliath in the valley below. My guess is that from up there the giant didn't look so big. But as David moved down and nearer, the giant seemed to get bigger and bigger, more threatening.

That's how our problems sometimes appear. The nearer they get the bigger and heavier we feel they are, but they're the same size really.

Someone imagined David's reaction as he saw the giant close up. His first thought was, "He's big !" but his next thought was, "I can't miss !"

Some of our problems are only as big as we make them and can be cut down to size with a bit of courage and the sort of trust in God that David had.

Sing to the Lord a new song, for he has done marvellous things; his right hand and his holy arm have worked salvation for him.

I've bought myself a new computer. I've had an old one for years and we'd grown used to each other but like me it was getting older and I thought it was time it went into honourable retirement.

My new one spent two days crouching on my desk growling at me and refusing to do any of the things I wanted it to do. Even the mouse wouldn't cooperate. Then, quite suddenly we became friends and a whole new world of possibilities opened up.

To start with it's fast and can do things my old one couldn't. Each time I play with it I sit back in amazement as I discover some new refinement. And in spite of doing so much more it does it all so much more easily – once you've got the hang of it.

But given a few weeks' use I know I'll start taking it for granted. All the surprise will disappear and it will become just another machine sitting there on my desk. The wonder of it will go and it will all become ordinary. A daily miracle reduced to the commonplace.

So much in life is miracle yet we are so used to it we accept it without a thought. Why should the sun rise every day? Why do the seasons follow one another in the same order every year? If only we could hold that sense of wonder life would sparkle again like it did when we were children. Above all, if only we could truly accept the wonder of God's love, life would be transformed quicker than any computer can do it.

Take a long look at your world today and open your mind to the miracles going on all around you.

The bird table

How many are your works, O Lord! In wisdom you made them all; the earth is full of your creatures.

I went to the vet the other day. Not for myself – I'm not quite as disillusioned with the National Health Service as that – I took one of our dogs. While I was waiting I picked up a leaflet – "Caring for Elderly Dogs".

The leaflet began by describing old dogs and the more I read the more it sounded like me. *"Greying round the muzzle"* – yes, that's me. *"Changes in body shape"* – I'm afraid so. *"Stiffness in the joints"* – certainly in my knees. *"Reluctance to take exercise"* – yes, I admit it. *"Bladder problems"*... I'll stop right there otherwise it might get a bit personal. And I know people say that dog owners get to look like their pets but that's taking it a bit far.

It made me think though. The similarities remind me that we humans are as much a part of God's creation as anything else and if we realised that we might begin to treat the earth and other living things a bit differently.

Of course we are different from animals in some ways – in being able to talk, to think, to imagine. And in our feelings for the spiritual. To wonder what life is about, and to realise there's more to it than just what we can see and measure. And that more is God, who created you and me, and my dogs, and wants the best for all of us.

And if we can begin to take that into account we may find it easier to live in harmony with each other, the world about us, and with the God who made us.

As water reflects a face, so a man's heart reflects the man.

I took my sketchbook and cycled down to the nature reserve near my home. It was a bright day, and a bit breezy. I stood at the edge of one of the lakes, watched the ripples on the water and tried to work out how I'd paint them.

The trouble was they kept changing colour. One moment the ripples looked sky blue, the next they were muddy brown. It's all a matter of reflection. The water's like a mirror; it reflects the blue sky when the angle's right, but when the angle changes, blown by the wind, you just see the muddy water. Both colours are true depending on your position.

In a way we all reflect what's going on around us. When life gets rough it shows in our attitudes and behaviour. It's the same with others. When someone's depressed or unresponsive maybe they're not just being bloodyminded, maybe something really is wrong and they need more understanding than we're prepared to give.

And when I find myself getting critical of other people and the way they are, perhaps if I changed my position slightly I might see them in a more favourable light. And when someone has a different point of view from mine maybe they're simply seeing things from a different angle.

**Do not merely listen to the word, and so deceive yourselves.
Do what it says.**

My family surprised me at Christmas. There'd been mysterious phone calls and a small parcel delivered next door but I'd no idea what it was all about. When I opened it on Christmas Day it was a voucher for a first lesson in flying a glider. The idea of soaring through the sky on a sunny day had appealed to me for a long time but I'd never done anything about it. Now here it was.

The voucher came with a couple of books on gliding which I quickly read from cover to cover. Now I know all about pre-flight checks to make sure the glider's safe and in working order. I know about winch launches and aero tows. About flaps and ailerons, rudder and elevators and what they do.

So, having read the books, I now know how to fly – how to take off, control the glider, and land safely.

That's the theory anyway. But come a sunny Spring day, when I actually sit in a glider with my instructor, I'm sure it'll all seem very different. Harder, more down to earth – although that's probably not the most appropriate phrase to use.

It's the difference between theory and practice. Between thinking and doing, between believing and actually living out what we believe. There's more to life than we can see and more to faith than simply talking about it. The proof comes not in sitting around reading but in putting it into practice.

Rhododendron wood

The body is a unit, though it is made up of many parts; and though all its parts are many, they form one body.

I waited impatiently for the winter to turn into Spring and produce a warm sunny day. I drove to the small airfield and there on the grass was a glittering silver two-seat glider. It was beautiful, a long sleek body with even longer slim wings. My instructor and I talked while he checked the aircraft. That seemed good sense.

The next bit I didn't like. He strapped a parachute harness on me and told me how to pull the cord if I should need to. The next bit I liked even less. As I shoe-horned myself into the forward seat he strapped me in tight. Tighter than tight. A harness over my shoulders, another across my lap, both locked together in the middle. I could move my head, my arms and legs but my body was immobile, fastened close to the seat. I felt trapped.

Once we were airborne though and freed from the towing plane, I understood. You become one with the glider. You move as part of it and not independently. When the glider banks you move with it. Everything it does, you do. You are not sitting in a machine that flies, you are flying, an integral part of it. It's the discipline which eventually adds to the experience, makes the enjoyment more intense.

In a very real sense one is "part of the body", not metaphorically but organically. And totally dependent on the pilot with you. I wouldn't have wanted to be freed from him or the glider. I was happy being one part of the whole and enjoying all that happened.

. . . but those who hope in the Lord will renew their strength.
They will soar on wings like eagles . . .

Before the glider took off it was quite useless. It had no engine, no means of getting into the air until a mechanic hooked us up by three hundred feet of cable to a light aircraft. A few hand signals later the plane was roaring down the runway with our glider bumping along behind it. Then we were airborne, but still dependent on the aircraft in front.

Once we'd achieved an altitude of a couple of thousand feet the instructor released the cable and we were on our own. Flying. After some instruction I was allowed to take the controls and fly the machine. It was magical. I was amazed how sensitive the controls were. Just a slight pressure on the control column and the glider's nose lifted, or sank, or we began to bank. I had thought it would take real strength, but gentleness was all that was needed.

As I began to get used to it there came a great sense of freedom as we moved around the air currents, but it was freedom with responsibility. We still had to watch the instrument panel, check the airspeed, altitude and rate of climb, and make sure we were not asking the glider to do things it couldn't do.

When we commit our lives as Christians we need the safety of a close tie with Jesus. We can only reach the heights closely attached to him. And it seems that all our decisions are made for us. But as we launch ourselves onto the winds of God's love, we find a new freedom which allows us to spread our wings and fly in the open spaces of his kingdom. Just remember that the controls are very sensitive.

"In my Father's house are many rooms . . ."

The other day I called in to see an exhibition of paintings at a local gallery. "Around the Garden" this one was called. A bit twee as a title but a lot of people paint flowers, and it was a colourful exhibition.

Some of the paintings were lively, even vigorous. Many concentrated on colour, others were detailed studies with every petal and stamen in place. One picture I remember had no flowers at all. The painter had been much more interested in the greenhouse at the bottom of the garden. Some of the pictures were abstract, others realistic.

Ask people to paint one subject and each one produces something quite different. Some see the whole thing, others concentrate on a single detail. To one accurate drawing's important, to another it's the broad effect that counts. Yet each one is true, each one gives a different viewpoint, a personal reaction.

That's life. We all see things a bit differently. We each react in our own way, and being different doesn't necessarily mean we're wrong. Or even that someone else is. We're just concentrating on different bits of the whole picture.

It would save a lot of aggro if we remembered that, and dropped the dogmatism; if we listened a bit more to other people and tried to understand what they're saying before we started to criticise them.

Maybe they too have a glimpse of the truth. And maybe it's just as valid as ours.

Flower market

"The Lord does not look at the things man looks at. Man looks at the outward appearance, but the Lord looks at the heart."

I love antique fairs. I'm a painter so I'm always on the lookout for interesting drawings or paintings. One day I'm going to find an unrecognised masterpiece by Turner. It's not happened yet but maybe next time?

Some time ago I bought an old Victorian oil painting. It was very dirty and had obviously been in a room above a smoky coal fire for years. It was covered in grime and stained dark brown. I could just make out a tree and a couple of sheep. I licked my finger and rubbed a bit. A branch of the tree began to show. It looked well painted so, after a bit of haggling, I took a risk and bought it.

Back home I went over the painting with a damp cloth and just a bit of soap. That got rid of some of the grime. Then, very carefully, I began to clean off the old varnish and bit by bit the picture began to show until the whole painting revealed itself.

It's not a great painting but it's a good one, and I can see it now the way the artist meant it to be. He painted it with love but over the years grime and smoke had dulled and darkened it.

Life can get heavy; overlaid with worry and routine. The beauty gets hidden under all our responsibilities. Maybe we need to shake off the dust, clean ourselves up, and live the way God meant us to be. And if we took a bit of time and trouble we might begin to recognise the possibilities in other people.

By faith Abraham, when called to go to a place he would later receive as his inheritance, obeyed and went, even though he did not know where he was going.

A s an artist, whenever I go into my studio and look at a blank sheet of watercolour paper I feel a mixture of excitement and anticipation. I see the paper's whiteness, its texture. It offers so many possibilities but I'm often reluctant to start painting. It could be the beginning of something good or a complete failure.

When I do begin, the first washes always feel good. That lovely blue running boldly across the sky, the texture of a cloud edge on the rough paper, the warm grey of its shadow. The way one colour runs into another.

Sometimes though it begins to go wrong. The more washes I put on the muddier it all gets. The more I try to correct it the more faults I see. I can't seem to realise my original idea. Yet another spoilt picture and disappointment. You should see the size of my waste-paper basket.

But there are times when everything goes well from the first wash to the finishing touches, including those happy accidents which artists accept with thanks and use in the painting. Accidents that Chinese artists call "gifts of God". Then the whole painting works and there's a feeling of great satisfaction.

The story of my life. Getting up each morning, looking forward to the day. A clean sheet in front of me. And what I make of it depends on what I put into it, what other people contribute and those happenings which are God's gift. And they're the most important, and the most reliable. In any case the day's an adventure, an exploration. Let's face it that way.

. . . and where the Spirit of the Lord is, there is freedom.

If Elvis Presley had lived he would be thinking about his pension now. The folk singer Bob Dylan said that hearing Elvis Presley playing rock and roll for the first time was "like busting out of jail".

Elvis Presley isn't everyone's first choice when it comes to music but what Dylan meant was that he'd been liberated – he'd heard music played like he'd never heard it played before. It had opened his mind to something new, offered him new ideas, given him a musical freedom he'd never had before.

It's easy to react to new ideas with a closed mind. To condemn without thinking, to seal ourselves off from all that makes life different. It's safer that way of course. You don't need to take risks, but it's less interesting.

Faith's meant to liberate, to free us from our hang-ups and fears, and give us something positive to live with. But, sad to say, we often try to protect our faith by closing our minds to new ideas. We pull what we know around us like a comfort blanket and refuse to listen.

Seeing a new church being built, an old aborigine asked, "If God loves everybody why do people build walls?" I'm not suggesting that we don't need church buildings but his question says to me that rather than sheltering inside the walls we build – whether they're made of brick or just walls in our minds – we should be out in the world with everyone else.

We may have to take risks, we may be exposed to music we've never listened to before, but we might just hear something new, gain something worth having.

Garden bouquet

"And do not set your heart on what you will eat or drink; do not worry about it. For the pagan world runs after all such things, and your Father knows that you need them. But seek his kingdom, and these things will be given to you as well."

Jedburgh Abbey is just across the border in Scotland. It's a lovely tranquil place. The ruined walls in warm red stone, their corners smoothed by centuries of wind and rain. A visitor once wrote:

"Everywhere peace, everywhere serenity, and a marvellous freedom from the tumult of the world."

The words have a modern ring to them but they were written 850 years ago. The longing for peace and quiet isn't new.

Walking around the ruins I tried to imagine what *"the tumult of the world"* really was all that time ago. The loudest noise then would have been a clap of thunder, the loudest human made noise church bells. No motorway traffic, no hi-fi at fifty watts playing through open summer windows.

But I guess it was the demands of everyday life that the writer was thinking of. The demands people made on his time, energy and sympathies. His daily routine and the occasional crisis.

Nothing much changes. They're the same demands on us today. Family concerns, the pressures of work or looking for work, meeting others' expectations. Most of us yearn for something different. We look back to an ideal past when we think life was quiet and peaceful. But it wasn't and we have to live in the now. Today is where we begin, and whether it's good or not, whether we like it or not, that's what we have to work with. We can only come to terms with the tumult of our world by facing it, not by wishing it away.

"In the same way, let your light shine before men, that they may see your good deeds and praise your Father in heaven."

S hortly before he died, Dennis Potter the playwright was interviewed for television. He had cancer of the liver and spleen and only had a few weeks to live. He was very positive. There was no self-pity, just an urge to live each day as it came, and to achieve all he could in the time he had left.

One thing he said really hit me. He said, *"Life can only be defined in the present tense."*

In other words today's what counts. He said he valued every minute. He saw things with new eyes. Looking at a plum tree blossoming he said it was *"the richest, whitest, blossomiest blossom"* he'd ever seen.

Today's what counts. Take that with you this morning. If you need to do something, say something to someone, do it today. If you want to achieve something start now.

I once went to Moscow in the days of the Soviet Union, before *glasnost.* I visited a Baptist Church there. The place was full, the choir superb. Afterwards I asked the leader how he got his singers so full of life and joy. "Every time we sing," he said, "it's with the thought that this may be the last time we'll ever be able to sing."

It wasn't a morbid thought, just a stimulus to use every minute to the full. I reckon if we lived life the same way we'd make the world sparkle more than it does.

"Do not let your hearts be troubled. Trust in God; trust also in me."

During the years I lived in India I had several chances to trek in the Himalayas. Once I was walking with a small medical team – a doctor and two paramedics with pack ponies – taking health care to village communities remote from ordinary life. Although the remoteness was ordinary life to the people there.

When you get tired walking in the mountains, you ride, particularly uphill. The trouble is all the animals are trained as pack ponies to carry baggage strapped each side of them. On narrow trails with rocks going up steeply on one side and with a sheer drop on the other the ponies all walk near the edge. Although it doesn't look it, it's safer that way because then the baggage doesn't catch on the rock face.

It's all right until you saddle up a pony to ride. It's usually docile enough but out of habit it still walks near the edge and you have to be pretty tired to ride with one leg dangling over a three hundred foot drop. You have to believe in the pony and trust it to put its feet just right. It's not always easy.

It's not always easy putting your faith in other people, but we all have to do it. We can't live in isolation. Wherever we are we have to trust somebody. The bus driver, the neighbour – someone. It can be hard, especially if we've been let down in the past but we have to do it. That's how we build relationships.

And it's the same with God. It can seem a pretty rocky idea trusting him, but it works. He doesn't let people down.

The old pasture

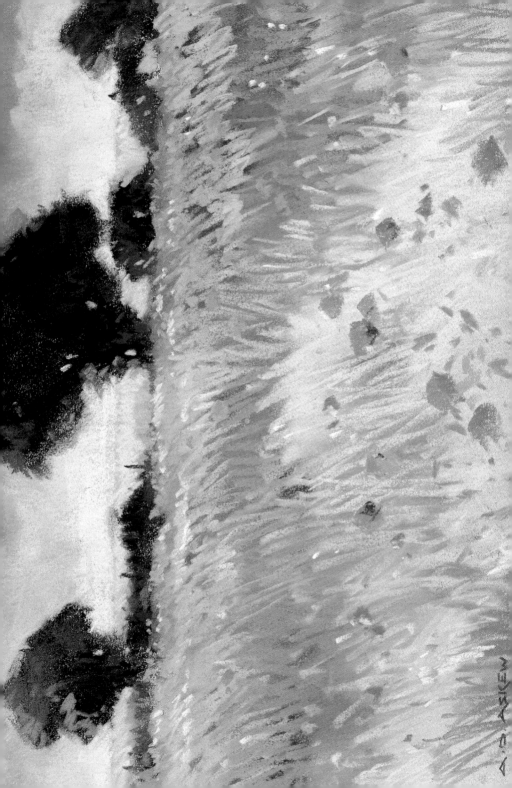

**I lift up my eyes to the hills – where does my help come from?
My help comes from the Lord, the Maker of heaven and earth.**

Walking in the Himalayas can be tough. The mountains are beautiful but they're hard going. Walking uphill is hard work but going downhill is worse. Harder on the knees. When you reach the top of a high ridge you find a rock to sit on. You tell your companions it's to admire the view but really it's to get your breath back and ease your calf muscles. And away in front of you is a great panorama of ridge after ridge, bluing off into the distance, lovely but remote.

Most of the time though your horizon's limited. You just walk with your eyes down, concentrating on the rocky path ahead and your next step. When you do look ahead all you see is the nearest rise, and happiness is getting to the next bend without stumbling. There are consolations. A waterfall, rushing stream, an ice cold drink of water from the glacier above.

Most of the time it's as well you can't see further. When you're getting tired you don't want to see too far. You're content just to keep on moving up the hill. But when you get there, when you hit the high point and look out over the distant mountains, all the sweat and aching legs are worthwhile. Something's been achieved, you've discovered a new viewpoint, won a little victory. It's something to treasure in your memory. And that's enough for the day.

"In your anger do not sin." Do not let the sun go down while you are still angry, and do not give the devil a foothold.

Lovely little animals, squirrels. All those acrobatics as they try to reach the peanuts we hang out for the birds in the garden. They usually manage it too. And take the lot.

But then they began to worry me. They started digging up and eating the tulip bulbs I'd planted in the autumn. I still forgave them. "Maybe I should have planted them deeper," I thought, but I wish now I'd done something to discourage them.

You see, the other day the burglar alarm went off for no apparent reason. I cleared it. Then it went off again, and again. Seven times in one afternoon. The engineer came, checked everything and found a broken wire in the loft. We looked at the wire more closely – toothmarks. Mice? Rats? No, a squirrel nesting in the loft and chewing through anything that got in its way.

I was told I'd better do something quick – the breeding season was beginning. I got onto a builder, but not before the squirrel had chewed through another wire and set the alarm off again. I won't bother you with the rest of the saga. The point is if I'd done something earlier about the squirrel the problem wouldn't have got so big. The word is "Act now." And that goes for human relationships, not just squirrels.

When friendships go wrong, when there are family misunderstandings, don't let them go on. Do something to put them right. Don't wait for the other person. Make a move yourself. The Bible says, *"Don't let the sun go down while you're still angry."* Do something to put things right. That way quarrels are short circuited, friendships restored. Don't go on shouting. Show a bit of love. But maybe not so much to the squirrels.

**But I trust in your unfailing love; my heart rejoices in your salvation.
I will sing to the Lord, for he has been good to me.**

I like to be in charge of things, particularly when they affect me. So when I went into hospital for surgery I began asking questions. I asked the surgeon just what he was going to do, and what complications there might be.

When the anaesthetist checked me over I asked how he'd give the anaesthetic and how I could expect to feel when I came round. I asked the sister if I'd wake up with a tube in my arm and whether there'd be any strange bits of plumbing I didn't usually carry around with me.

Some folk don't want to know these details but the more I know the better I feel. Yet however much of a manager you are there are times when you just have to surrender control to other people.

It's all a question of trust, especially in hospital. And not only there. Outside in the ordinary world too. For some that's easier said than done. I'm lucky, my trust hasn't been abused like some folks' has. But you can only live in relationships by trusting. Of course you must ask questions, but in the end you have to trust.

And as I went down into the operating theatre some words of an old saint came to mind. In one of her visions Jesus said to Mother Julian of Norwich, *"And all shall be well, and all shall be well, and all manner of things shall be well."* It didn't mean that everything would instantly, magically, be all right but that whatever happened you could trust God to be in it with you, helping you cope, and promising that in one way or another, he'd bring something good out of it.

A neglected border

. . . in humility consider others better than yourselves. Each of you should look not only to your own interests, but also to the interest of others.

As she came through the door the nurse asked, "How are you this morning?" Then the sister came. "What sort of a night did you have? Did you get any sleep?" An hour later the surgeon came in and asked, "How are you feeling today. Everything going all right?"

And so it went on through the day. My wife, my minister, other visitors. All concerned, caring, following my progress, either as professionals or friends. All questions about me, my health.

Pretty gratifying in one sense but there was a down side to it, because it all encouraged me to concentrate on myself. Everything that happened in hospital seemed to revolve round me. And when anyone came into my room it was very easy to slip into the habit of talking about myself and nothing else. Once I realised what was happening, whenever anyone came I tried to be first in asking how *they* were, and tried to listen to the answer.

Centring your life on yourself isn't a very good idea. It makes you too selfish. You've got to get hold of something else, some other purpose, and look outwards. As Saint Paul, said, *"Look not only to your own interests but also to the interests of others."* It's not always easy to do it, but when Paul wrote that he was in prison for his faith, and that's a lot worse than being in hospital.

"On the third day he will rise again."

I watched a beech tree for three days. It was outside my room in the hospital. There wasn't much else to see and when the only other thing you can do all day is read, sleep or listen to the radio a beech tree becomes very interesting.

It was a beautiful tree, its tall, elegant, silver-grey trunk powdered with green lichen. And it moved. Its branches swayed in the wind. Over those three days I watched its hard tight buds develop into crinkly leaves just beginning to show that light bright green that makes Spring come alive. It was a lovely sight.

The tree had been pruned at some time. A couple of branches had been taken off but smooth calluses had grown over the wounds, and they too were beautiful in a way. That was reassuring after surgery. And as I watched, the tree began to talk to me. No, it wasn't the late effects of the anaesthetic. It said to me, "You know, whatever's happening to you the world's still out here, quietly getting on with life. The sun comes up each morning, the rain comes down most afternoons" – it was April after all – "and nature's doing its own thing."

It also reassured me that something, someone, somewhere is still in charge. That there's a power for good which we call God at work, creating, sustaining, shaping and restoring our world, our lives. And if that sometimes involves a bit of pruning, so be it.

The beech tree also reminded me that nothing stays the same. That in three days buds turn to leaves, and that in three days new life can become a reality. Just as it did at Easter.

. . . you also, like living stones, are being built into a spiritual house to be a holy priesthood, offering spiritual sacrifices acceptable to God through Jesus Christ.

On holiday I walked along part of Hadrian's Wall in Northumberland. The Romans built it when Britain was part of the Roman Empire. I say the Romans built it – I expect it was local folk who did most of the hard work, the Romans just got the credit. What's new?

It's still impressive nearly two thousand years later. A great, grey stone wall following the rise and fall of the hills, its length dotted with turrets and little forts.

At Housesteads we wandered through the excavations of the fortress, through the barracks and the bath house, the hospital and the communal loo. It made me smile to see the commandant's villa set next to the southern gate, as far away from the actual wall as possible. Maybe a commander has to be behind his troops, but he'd also be at the nearest point for a sharp exit in time of trouble. Maybe I'm just a bit cynical.

In the museum there are things that remind you of the human side of life on the Wall. Memorial stones dedicated to one of the many Roman gods or carved with the names of people who'd died. People hoping to be remembered, hoping to leave something behind them.

What would I leave behind, I wondered? I wasn't thinking of stone walls or carved memorials, I was thinking more of relationships. What will each of us leave behind today? As we go through the day, do our work, meet people and build relationships, how will the day appear when we look back at it? If we've made somebody feel good, feel better for having been with us, that'll be more valuable than any stone memorial.

Spring colours

You know that the testing of your faith develops perseverance. Perseverance must finish its work so that you may be mature and complete, not lacking anything.

The great French Romantic painter Eugene Delacroix was producing his masterpieces early in the 19th Century. It's said that he had a cleaning woman who regularly visited his studio to tidy up. She often watched him at work painting.

Eventually she made her pronouncement. "Painting's easy," she said, "All you have to do is put the right colour in the right place." That's one way of summing up the art of painting but few artists would agree that that was all. Knowing what the right colour is, how to mix it and exactly where it should go on the canvas is hard enough, but releasing the power of feeling and imagination for the initial inspiration is even more demanding. And that's what turns a painter into an artist.

Using similar reasoning we could say, "Living out the Christian life is easy. All it takes is the ability to do the right thing at the right time." Easily said. The problem comes in doing it. In finding the courage to live out the faith in practical ways, and taking every opportunity that comes. It isn't just a matter of mechanics or organisation, it needs to be based on something deeper.

As artists draw their inspiration from deep inside themselves, the Christian has to draw on that source of strength we call the Holy Spirit, present within us and trying all the time to move us into greater creativity in our relationships.